A McGRAW-HILL NATURAL SCIENCE PICTURE BOOK

Scientific Adviser: Dr. Gwynne Vevers
Curator of the Aquarium, The Zoological Society of London

Animals of the Desert

J. L. CLOUDSLEY-THOMPSON

ILLUSTRATED BY

COLIN THREADGALL

McGRAW-HILL BOOK COMPANY
NEW YORK · ST. LOUIS · SAN FRANCISCO

McGRAW-HILL NATURAL SCIENCE PICTURE BOOKS

ANIMAL LIFE IN THE ANTARCTIC by Dr. F. D. Ommanney

ANIMALS OF THE ARCTIC by Dr. Gwynne Vevers
Curator of the Aquarium, The Zoological Society of London

ANTS AND TERMITES by Dr. Gwynne Vevers

APES AND MONKEYS by Dr. Desmond Morris

BATS by Dr. David Pye

THE BIG CATS by Dr. Desmond Morris

THE CURIOUS WORLD OF SNAKES by Alfred Leutscher
Co-founder and first Secretary, British Herpetological Society

LIFE IN THE SEA by Dr. Gwynne Vevers

ELEPHANTS AND MAMMOTHS by Dr. Gwynne Vevers

THE ORIGINS OF MAN by Dr. John Napier
Director of Primate Biology Program, Smithsonian Institution, Washington, D.C.

PLANTS THAT EAT ANIMALS by Dr. Linna Bentley
Lecturer in Botany, Bedford College, University of London

THE SMALL WATER MAMMALS by Maxwell Knight

THE STARS by Colin A. Ronan

ANIMALS OF THE DESERT

First distribution in the United States of America by
McGraw-Hill Book Company, 1971

First published in Great Britain by
The Bodley Head, Ltd., 1969
Library of Congress Catalog Card Number: 73-155172
Printed in Great Britain

Contents

Deserts, 5

Climate, soil, and vegetation, 6

Camels, 8

Asses and kangaroos, 10

Antelopes, 13

Kit-foxes, fennecs, and rats, 14

Hares and ground squirrels, 16

Gerbils, jerboas, and kangaroo rats, 18

Ostriches and other birds, 20

Lizards and turtles, 22

Snakes, 24

Scorpions and camel spiders, 27

Insects, woodlice, and centipedes, 28

Oases, 30

Nomads, 32

TURKESTA
DESERT
NORTH
AMERICAN
DESERT
IRANIAN
DESERT
INI
DE
TROPIC OF
CANCER
ARABIAN
DESERT
SAHARA DESERT
EQUATOR
ATACAMA DESERT
NAMIB DESERT
TROPIC OF
CAPRICORN
KALAHARI
DESERT
PATAGONIAN DESERT

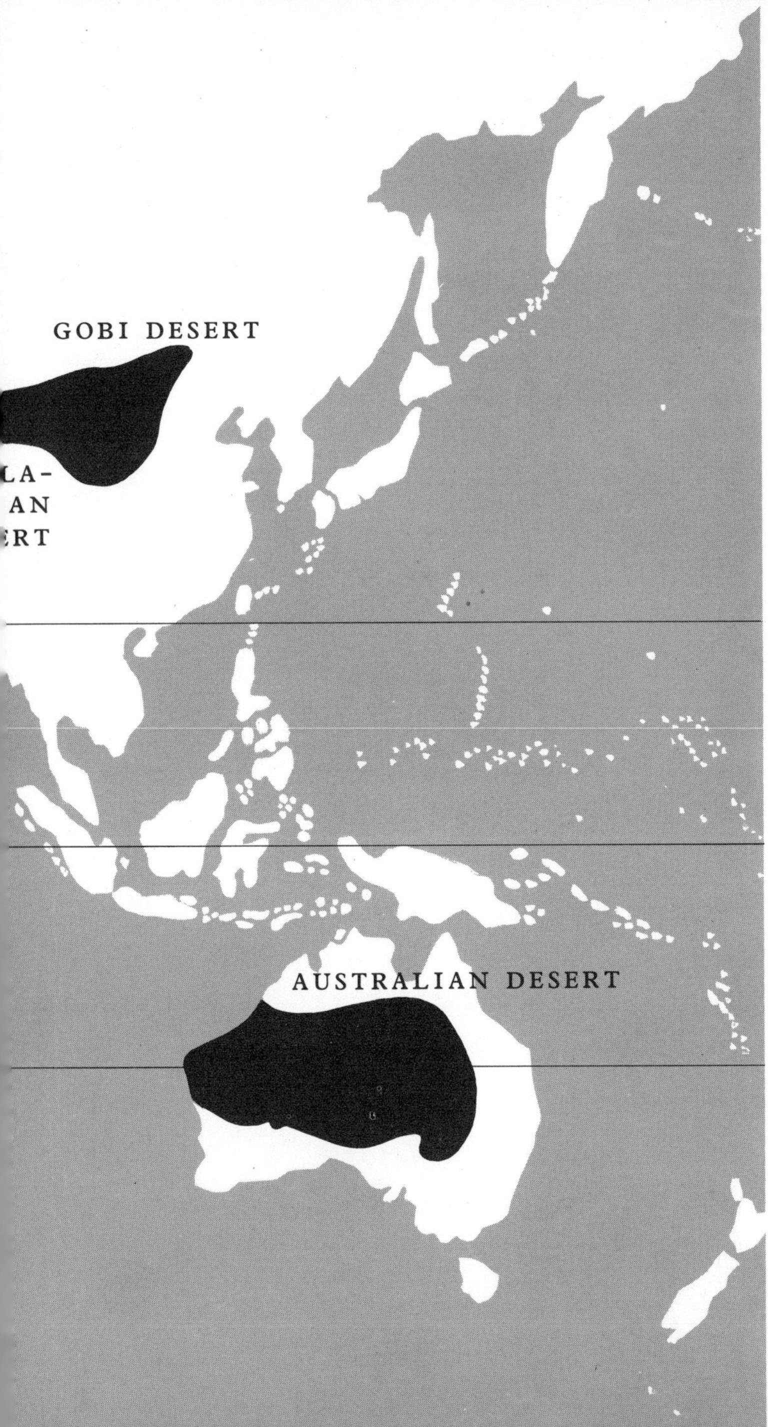

Deserts

Nearly one fifth of the land surface of the world is occupied by desert and semi-desert. The map shows the most important of these desert areas. The largest is the Great Palaearctic Desert which includes the Sahara, Arabian, Iranian, Turkestan, Indian, Takla-Makan, and Gobi Deserts. This vast desert region stretches almost continuously across North Africa and Asia Minor into India and the center of China. The Sahara alone covers $3\frac{1}{2}$ million square miles. Next in size come the Australian Desert ($1\frac{1}{3}$ million square miles), the Great American Desert (500,000 square miles), the Kalahari and Namib Deserts of South Africa, and the Atacama and Patagonian Deserts.

The deserts of the world tend to lie near the tropics. The hottest part of the world is between the two parallels of latitude marked on the map as the tropic of Cancer and the tropic of Capricorn.

Climate, soil, and vegetation

For most of the year the desert is dry and barren. The days, especially in summer, are extremely hot and a scorching sun blazes in the sky. By contrast, the nights are cold because there are no clouds to blanket the earth. Rain is scarce and when it does fall at certain times of the year, it usually comes in violent thunderstorms separated by periods of dry weather. Most of the water runs away so rapidly, however, that only a little of it sinks into the ground. Desert water courses are dry throughout most of the year, but may become raging torrents for one or two days. They are known as *wadis* and in America as *arroyos*.

The desert air is very dry and strong winds often blow, carrying with them small particles of dust and sand which scour and erode the rocks, sometimes producing very weird shapes. Sand storms are common. Larger grains of sand form dunes which are blown slowly across the surface of the desert. Desert sand becomes so smooth and polished that it does not hurt when it blows into one's eyes. It is far less gritty than sea sand when it gets into food. Not all deserts are sandy, however. Many deserts are rocky or stony, and some are formed of clay.

Although deserts are so dry, there are usually a few flowering plants in the less arid parts. For example, in the desert of Southern California, shown in the drawing, evening primroses blossom in the spring. Arizona is famous for wild flowers, and the spring rains bring forth an abundance of color in the desert regions around the Mediterranean.

Many of these plants only appear after rain and spend the rest of the year as seeds buried in the ground. Others, like cactuses, store water in their stems. Many of the trees drop their leaves during the dry season. Desert shrubs usually have sharp and prickly thorns which protect them from browsing animals. They often secrete poisonous chemical substances which make their leaves taste bitter.

Camels

Camels live very well in the desert because they can go for a long time without water. Their urine is very concentrated and little water is lost with their droppings, so they can get rid of waste products from their bodies without using up too much precious water. The hump is a food store which helps them in the dry season when they cannot get enough to eat. This food reserve is in the form of fat. If this fat were spread all over the body, it would act as a blanket and make the camel hot.

Our body temperature keeps the same (98·6° F.) all the time, except when we have a fever; but the body of the camel gets hotter and hotter during the day. This heat is stored until the night comes and the air becomes cooler. Then the camel becomes cooler, too. Only when its temperature has risen to 105·3° F. does the camel begin to sweat. By allowing its body temperature to rise, the camel is able to save a lot of water. This would be lost as sweat if camels had to keep a steady temperature all the time as we do. The camel's hair is very coarse so that, when the animal does have to sweat, the water evaporates on its skin where the cooling effect is most useful.

The Arabian camel or dromedary (right) has a single hump and short hair on its flanks and belly; while the two-humped Bactrian camel (left), which inhabits the deserts of central Asia where the winters are very cold, grows a long winter coat.

Both kinds of camel have fleshy pads on their feet which prevent them from sinking into soft sand, and callouses to rest on when they are kneeling. Their eyes have long lashes which protect them from flying sand and dust.

Although they grumble when being loaded, camels are docile creatures (except at the mating season). They are so important to the nomads of the Great Palaearctic Desert that there are about 150 words in the Arabic language to describe them according to their age, color, and other characteristics.

Asses and kangaroos

After the camel, the largest animals of the desert are domesticated donkeys and wild asses. These are sure-footed creatures with long ears. They, too, can live without water for several days and, like camels, they do not lose their appetites even when they get thirsty. Nevertheless, they lose water more rapidly than camels do. The variations in their body temperature are smaller, so they have to sweat more. Also their fur coats are thinner and do not protect them so well from the hot sun. When they do get a chance to drink, donkeys and asses can take in amazing quantities of water.

There are several different kinds of wild asses. The onager of central Asia is the wild ass of the Bible. It is white, with a large yellowish area on its sides and a black mane and tail. It moves in herds led by an old stallion. The kiang, which inhabits the high deserts of Tibet, Ladak, and Sikkim, is a deep reddish brown, and is more solitary in its habits. The kulan of southern Russia and the Gobi Desert (left) is smaller and brownish or sandy-colored. Wild asses are also found in Somalia and the Nubian Desert of Africa.

Kangaroos range widely throughout the inland desert regions of Australia. Most of their water comes with their vegetarian diet and they can survive with only occasional drinking. They move very quickly by jumping. The body is carried well forward and balanced by the heavy tail. The red kangaroo (right) is perhaps the best known species. As in all marsupial animals, the young are born in a comparatively unformed state. They climb up into their mother's pouch or *marsupium*, where they complete their development. The young 'joey' in the picture is old enough to leave his mother for short periods when all is safe. But even quite large 'joeys' shelter in their mother's pouch when danger threatens or when they are tired.

Antelopes

Antelopes keep cool in the desert by hiding during the daytime in the shade of rocks and bushes, so that they do not need to sweat much. Most of their water is taken in with their food. In many places they do not drink at all, because they can get enough moisture from succulent leaves and roots.

Dorcas gazelles are small antelopes found throughout the Sahara and Middle East Deserts. They are very speedy, and when necessary will travel long distances to get food or drinking water. They like to browse on acacia trees.

Various kinds of oryx antelope are found throughout the deserts and plains of Africa south of the Sahara, Arabia, and Iraq. The Arabian oryx is the smallest. It is dirty white in color, with long, scimitar-like horns. The gemsbok of South-East Africa is found in less arid country. The beisa of East Africa and Ethiopia has the most striking coloration of all: it is brown, white, and black.

Oryx are formidable creatures when annoyed. They charge with lowered heads, thrusting their horns from side to side and screaming through their noses. The addax antelope is smaller and weaker, but it is even more independent of water, so it can exist in the drier and more remote parts of the Sahara.

The odd-looking Saiga antelope of Western Asia shown in the drawing has a long, swollen nose with nostrils set far back so that sand does not get in while the animal is grazing. It is fast and travels very far to get water.

Kit-foxes, fennecs, and rats

The delicate kit-foxes of North America and the fennec fox of the Sahara look very much alike and have big ears. They are all much smaller than foxes from cooler and wetter countries. They spend the daytime in deep burrows, thus avoiding extremes of heat. Like most other desert animals they are a pale, sandy color. The drawing shows an American bobcat stalking a kit-fox which is itself hunting kangaroo rats. If the bobcat were chased by a jaguar it could escape by climbing up a giant cactus!

The fennec eats more different kinds of food than other foxes, for it must do this if it is to survive in the desert. It feeds mainly on insects, lizards, mice, and dates. Indeed, its liking for sweet things explains the fable of the fox and the grapes. (English foxes do not like grapes.) The cubs are born in burrows at the time of the rains when there is more food available.

Fennecs and kit-foxes get most if not all of their water from their food and produce very salty urine. If they do get overheated, they pant like dogs, but normally they keep in the shade of their burrows during the day. Some other desert animals, like the grasshopper mice of North America and the Australian mulgara which eat juicy insects, do not drink at all. They get enough water with their food and produce very strong urine as the foxes do. The sand rats of North Africa, on the other hand, live and nest in places where there are succulent plants, which are usually extremely salty. Sand rats eat these in great quantities and get rid of the salt in their urine which may be four times as salty as sea water.

Hares and ground squirrels

Many kinds of hares live in less extreme deserts. They are small but very speedy, and pale in color, so that they cannot easily be seen by enemies such as foxes and bobcats. Most of them dig tunnels and burrows to live in, but the American jack rabbit (left) always remains above ground. These jack rabbits live in places where there is no water and depend upon the moisture in the green food that they eat. Like the Saharan hare, they have very long ears which help to cool their blood. Many other desert animals, including the fennecs and kit-foxes, have large ears which help to cool their bodies.

Ground squirrels (right) are found in many desert regions. They spend the hot part of the day in deep, cool burrows, coming out only in the early morning and the cool of the evening. During very hot, dry weather, when there is no food for them, they do not come out at all. They aestivate in their burrows and go into a state of torpor in the summer in the same way that English squirrels hibernate in the winter. Their body temperature then drops to that of the air in the burrows which is comparatively cool. At the same time they breathe very slowly so that they lose little moisture from their lungs.

Another desert animal which aestivates during the dry season is the poor-will, which inhabits the California deserts. It is the only kind of bird known to aestivate, and as no birds hibernate, this is of great interest to biologists.

Related to the ground squirrels are the prairie dogs of North America. These rodents are more than a foot in length when adult and weigh about 2 lb. Their fur is reddish-brown above and light beneath. They live in large colonies and recognize each other by making hissing sounds. They dig their burrows in grassy plains and share them in a friendly way with rattlesnakes and ground owls. The rattlesnakes never bite them.

Gerbils, jerboas, and kangaroo rats

The desert is a harsh place for animals to live in, because the days are very hot and there is little water. That is why so many desert animals spend the days in deep burrows in the ground. Gerbils, jerboas, and kangaroo rats are small, mouse-like animals. They live in holes in the ground and come out only at night, except in winter when the days are cooler. They form the staple food of most desert predators, being preyed on by foxes, mongooses, eagles, kites, snakes, and monitor lizards. Their own food consists mainly of vegetable matter, especially seeds.

The jerboas of Asia and Africa and the kangaroo rats of America have long back legs and can move very fast by jumping, like real kangaroos. The drawing on the left shows a pygmy jerboa from Baluchistan which is only $1\frac{1}{2}$ inches long. The Mongolian gerbil illustrated on the right is a species which lives well in captivity and is becoming a popular pet.

These animals can live indefinitely on dry food. Very little water is used for excretion, and their urine is very concentrated. The air in their burrows is cool and damp so that they do not lose much water vapor in their breathing. They do not sweat. They are so small that they could not afford to do so, for the surface area of their bodies is so large in comparison with their weight that they would lose too much moisture if they cooled their bodies in this way.

If a kangaroo rat does get too hot it produces a lot of saliva. This wets the fur of its chin and throat so that its body is cooled by evaporation. Of course, it cannot do this for very long. It is an emergency process which might help if a rat were driven out of its burrow by an enemy such as a snake. For a short time it prevents death from overheating, but the kangaroo rat must find shelter very quickly.

Ostriches and other birds

Compared with reptiles and small mammals, birds are scarce in the desert. This is because birds are mostly active during the day. They cannot burrow, so they have to keep cool by panting. The evaporation of moisture in their breath cools the tissues of their lungs and the blood circulating through them. Birds do not sweat. Panting uses up a lot of water in evaporation, so most birds must be able to fly to water to drink.

Sand-grouse fly many miles to water each morning. They nest far away from lakes and rivers. Before he drinks, the father bird rubs his breast on the ground. This ruffles his feathers so that they are soaked in water while he is drinking. Then he flies back to the nest. The babies suck the water from his feathers with their beaks. They keep changing places until it is all used up.

Birds have higher body temperatures than mammals. This helps them in the desert, because they can lose heat without panting unless the weather is very hot. The American mourning dove can let its body temperature get very high before it begins to pant, in the same way that the camel gets very hot before it begins to sweat. This saves water.

Large flying birds such as eagles and vultures soar in the cooler, upper air during the day, while smaller birds such as larks and chats shelter in bushes or the shade of rocks.

The ostrich is far too big to take shelter and

cannot fly, although it travels very fast for long distances. Ostriches can drink salt water because they have special glands in their noses which get rid of the extra salt that enters the body. Like the camel, the ostrich can lose much of its body water without ill effect. When this happens, its body temperature begins to rise. Excess heat is then lost from the naked body and legs. As the drawing shows, the ostrich has feathers only on the back and wings.

Lizards and turtles

Lizards and turtles are reptiles. Reptiles do not keep their body temperatures as steady as birds and mammals do. When the weather is cold, they warm themselves in the sun; when it is hot, they hide in holes or cracks in the rocks. Their bodies are covered with dry scales and they do not sweat.

Lizards are very common in deserts. Most of them feed on insects, and many of them have salt glands in their noses through which they can get rid of surplus salt. They do not usually need to drink, because they can get enough water from the blood of the insects they eat.

Lizards that live in sandy deserts often have a fringe of scales on their toes, which prevents their feet from sinking into soft

sand. Some of them have valves in their noses which stop the sand from getting in. A few of them have a window in their lower eyelid so that they can see even when their eyes are shut to keep the sand out. Most geckos are able to climb rocks, trees, and walls by means of the special pads on their toes. The banded gecko shown in the drawing is found from Southern Texas to California and Mexico and is about $3\frac{1}{2}$ inches long. It has claws on its feet instead of pads, and a stout tail which it waves in a threat display when disturbed.

Like lizards, desert turtles avoid the heat by burrowing in the ground. They scrape the soil with their strong legs and push it away with their shells. They bury their eggs in the same way. They get moisture from the sap of the plants they feed on.

When turtles get too hot, saliva comes out of their mouths and noses and covers their heads, necks, and front legs. This cools them.

Snakes

Many people do not like snakes, but most of these reptiles are harmless and can become very tame if they are treated kindly. Even poisonous snakes can be quite friendly. Snakes are much less common than lizards. Most desert snakes prey on jerboas and kangaroo rats and get all their moisture from the blood of their prey. They do not chew their food, but swallow it whole. Their jaws can open very wide to let them do this. Snakes follow their prey by smell, and desert rattlesnakes can detect the warmth of their prey up to a distance of 18 inches.

Snakes cannot survive high temperatures as well as lizards, so they have to hide away in cool places during the day. Some of them burrow in the ground and move by winding themselves sideways through the sand, as the African horned viper (left) is doing.

There are three kinds of poisonous snakes. The first includes the vipers and rattlesnakes. Their long fangs are placed at the front of the mouth and the snake stabs when it strikes. The fangs are folded back when not in use. The American diamondback rattlesnake (right) is in the defensive posture which it adopts when about to strike.

The second group of poisonous snakes includes the kraits, cobras, and mambas. In

these, the poison fangs cannot be folded back.

The back-fanged snakes which form the third group are less dangerous because they cannot inject poison into anything not actually in their mouths. They are related to grass snakes which are not poisonous.

Snakes usually warn people to keep away from them by hissing. Rattlesnakes make an angry buzzing noise by vibrating their rattles. These are made up of horny pieces of dry skin at the end of the tail. Snakes do not bite people unless they are frightened or harmed. Their poison is meant for killing their prey and it helps in digestion. So it is merely bad luck to be bitten by a poisonous snake, and there is no need to be frightened of them. Just take care not to tread on one!

Scorpions and camel spiders

Scorpions and camel spiders—like spiders, harvest spiders, and mites—are arachnids. These have four pairs of legs as well as a pair of claws or palps.

Most scorpions are very much at home in the desert, but some kinds live only in damp places. These are the big black scorpions of the rain forest, which are not very poisonous. Desert scorpions are mostly yellow and live under rocks and stones, or dig deep burrows with their claws. They vary in size from about 1 to 5 inches in length and come out only at night. Although they have poisonous stings at the end of their tails, they would soon be eaten by storks and other birds if they crawled about during the day. They use their poison to help them kill insect prey, and only sting people who hurt them by mistake. In some the poison is dangerous, but many species can cause only pain to a man. Some scorpions hiss like snakes when disturbed, and this warns people to leave them alone.

Baby scorpions are born alive because the eggs are retained in the mother's body until they are ready to hatch. The young scorpions ride on their mother's back until they are old enough to look after themselves. Scorpions feed on insects and eat each other too, when they get an opportunity. They do not often drink, but make do with the blood of their prey.

Camel spiders, sun spiders, or 'jerrymanders' are very strong for their size. Most of them are bigger than real spiders and have long legs. (The species illustrated has been only slightly enlarged by the artist.) They are very hairy and run so fast that they look like balls of thistledown blowing across the desert. Most of them hide away in deep holes or under stones during the daytime. They feed on insects and scorpions and are extremely greedy. If a big one catches a scorpion, it chews it up in no time. Camel spiders will go on eating and eating until they can scarcely move. Although they have immensely strong jaws, they are not poisonous.

Insects, woodlice, and centipedes

Many types of insect are found in the desert. Swarms of desert locusts are blown for hundreds of miles in the upper air. They land where rain has fallen and fresh green grass is growing. Here they feed and lay their eggs.

The 'manna' which the Children of Israel ate during their wanderings in Sinai is the sweet secretion of a bug which sucks the juices of plants. Flies, wasps, ants, and termites do well in the desert, too. But most successful of all are big, black desert beetles. Some of these come out only at night, but others are active during the hottest part of the day.

The scarab beetle makes a ball of camel dung which she rolls across the desert (as shown on the right of the drawing). Then she buries the treasure and lays her eggs on it. Darkling beetles (left of drawing) are wingless. They are very tough, and can live for years without food or water. They can withstand high temperatures and eat almost any plant or animal material that they find.

Their black color is a warning to other animals that they are not good to eat, for they are extremely hard, have a bad taste, and produce an unpleasant smell.

Desert woodlice or sow bugs live in oases and the beds of *wadis* where they help each other to dig deep burrows in the sand. Many woodlice live in each burrow. They have long legs to hold their bodies above the hot sand and do not come out of their holes until evening.

The centipedes of deserts are also burrowing types. Some of them are very long and have more legs than even a big millipede. Insects have only six legs, arachnids have eight, but woodlice have seven pairs and centipedes many more.

Oases

Oases are fertile places where there is water in the middle of the desert. In many oases of North Africa and America the water comes from underground. Other oases get their water from rivers which flow from mountains. Ribbon-like oases are found along the banks of the Rio Grande, Colorado, Indus, Tigris, and Euphrates. The Nile valley is the largest oasis of this kind in the world. Tamanrasset and Tibesti in the central Sahara are oases on high mountain plateaus where rain falls.

Desert oases often support towns and even great cities, because they are so fertile. Many, such as Cairo, Omdurman, Kano, and Palmyra, have played important roles in history.

Many kinds of animals live in oases because there is food and water there. Animals from the desert come into oases at night to

drink, and birds flying across the desert often stop at oases to feed. Many beautiful date palms grow in the oases of the Great Palaearctic Desert, and farmers cultivate various crops beneath their shade. All these plants provide food for insects and other animals.

At night the air is filled with the songs and chirrups of grasshoppers and crickets.

Dragonflies, and other insects that live in water for a part of their life, are common. Frogs and toads also live successfully in oases, because they lay their eggs in water. Their tadpoles live in water, too. Because oases are so fertile, many people live in them with their sheep, goats, donkeys, and camels. Camel caravans still cross the desert from one oasis to another, but they are being replaced by trucks which are far less exciting to watch.

Nomads

Some people live settled lives in oases where they cultivate dates and other crops, but true desert-dwellers are nomads, who wander from place to place with their goats and camels.

The nomadic bushmen of the Kalahari Desert are cunning hunters and magnificent archers. They can hit a moving antelope with a poisoned arrow at a range of 150 yards. (In the drawing they are taking aim at a gemsbok antelope.)

The Bushmen of Africa store water for the dry season in ostrich egg shells and gourds. In times of plenty their buttocks grow fat, but they shrink during hungry periods. Bushmen are very shy, but they are intelligent, cheerful, and good-natured.

Life is very hard for people who live in deserts, but they like it. I know one man who was a judge and very rich. When he became old, he retired and gave away his money. Then he went back to his tribe to be a nomad in the desert. He lived as he had when he was a little boy, with just a camel, a few goats, and his friends. And he was happy.